# *Palomino Plumes*

## REEMA GHOSH MAJUMDAR

PALOMINO PLUMES

**First published in 2020 by**

**Becomeshakespeare.com**

One Point Six Technologies Pvt Ltd.

119-123, 1st Floor, Building J2, B - Wing, WadalaTruck Terminal, Wadala East, Mumbai, Maharashtra, India, 400022.T:+91 8080226699

WORDIT ART FUND

This book has been partially funded by the Wordit Art Fund
Wordit Art Fund helps deserving authors publish
their work by providing monetary support
To apply for funding, please visit us at
www.BecomeShakespeare.com



ISBN - 978-93-90266-97-5

# DEDICATION

*To Maa and Bapi*

# ACKNOWLEDGMENTS

RUDRAKSHI GHOSH, my younger daughter, for complete technical support in compilation of the book. Her relentless effort in typing and editing shaped the book into what it is today.

RUDRANI GHOSH, my elder daughter for literally forcing me to show the sunlight to my hidden gems. Being a budding designer herself, she took care of the aesthetic aspects of the book. And has been the best critic too.

GAUTAM MAJUMDAR, my good friend and mentor, for making me believe that 'You can't beat a person who won't give up'.

Last but not the least, my husband SANJAY GHOSH, a man who is miles away from literature, being the biggest fan of my writings, and has been inspiring me to write since the day I met him.

# PALOMINO PLUMES

# CONTENTS

# DREAMS

## 101

I will emerge as a writer,
The day my velocity of enthusiasm
Surpasses the reader's impetus.
The day I rise way above earthly
Accolades and veneration.

The day my words would inspire universally,
My ilk, my pattern would get etched in memories.

The day I read my own creation
And turn the grey into million shades brighter,
That day, I shall truly emerge as a writer.

# 102

You live up to your name
My Acacia tree.
Rooted deep inside,
Spreading your branches
To shade from unavoidable scorching heat,
Sheltering whenever the droplets of rain fall
Swaying my emotions on a rollercoaster ride through your
lush leaves
Firm on the ground of my soul
Standing tall in every season
Unfolding various colors of life and love
Your healing properties nullifies all hurt..
The only grievance your grandeur cannot fit into my little
courtyard.

From far I would cherish
From distance would forever love.

# 103

Once Love whispered near my shoulders
A melodious interlude
It kept on crawling up and down my spine thereafter.

The other day love slipped from a hive and stung
Hard on my lips
Till now my lips are chanting the celestial buzz.

One day Love would definitely invite
For a rainbow dance and I would be stuck
Somewhere between my spine and my lips.

# 104

Often I wish I could just lie down and worry about
nothing.
Often I pray I wake up to my solitary magnanimous
dream,
Where sunbeam falls on my grey strand of hair
And the gurgle of a nearby stream
Adds rhythm to my ears.
I see robins nestling on my canopy
And I feel your breathe just beside me,
Curled up on my lap you sleep satiated
I rub your shoulders and kiss your forehead.

## 105

There is an urgent urge
To write about you
My darling muse.
Encircling in my mind is
Your myriad gestures
Your unique patterns and hues,
Your enchanting ways
Paving roads on my heart.
My mystical knight,
Your laughter is my armor,
Your songs are my shield,
You are my eternal light!

# 106

Togetherness of hearts
Has its own proximity.
Closeness encloses hearts
To a different realm,
Physical boundaries,
Take a leap from gravity
Mingling amicably
With the ethereal air
To experience a riot on the sensibilities.
Nothing would estrange the entwined hearts...

# 107

Love is magic,
In embraces of togetherness.
Love is curse,
In enduring estrangement.

Love is fact
In its history and insignias.
Love is myth
In star gazing dilemmas.

Love is gift
In smiles and happiness.
Love is gullible
In fear and business.

Love is freedom
In acceptance and seals;
Love is bondage
In distance and deals.

Love is eternal
In souls forlorn

Love is transient
In moments unknown.

Love is music
In lament and sighs;
Love is silence
In heart wrenching cries.

# 108

An invincible desire to sleep in your arms
My unkempt locks tenderly sorted
Strands one by one removed from my forehead
And a kiss so soft planted
With much love and affection.
I close my eyes,
And you keep stroking
Gently my cheeks.
My crown, my shoulders, my neck
Caress me tight on your heaving chest
Your heartbeats chime like lullabies
And I drift to a soothing slow slumber.
I wish,
My perfect idea
Of a peaceful sleep
Comes true some day.
Even if for once.

# 109

I go down to my velvet underground
Where I profoundly cover myself with sighs,
The wax melts from my wings
Just can't bear the fights.
For powerless I am
In shielding my feels for you
My horrible demons diminishes only
When you whisper,
I love you.

110

You are the gentle southern breeze which passes through the
flora of my window curtain and plants a
Feathery kiss on my closed eyelid whispering into my ears the
most adorable endearments,
I wake up with you.

You are variant spices in my kitchen peeping through each
jar and guiding me to bring you out in right proportion to
enhance my culinary delights with your lingering aroma
intoxicating my gut till my inner soul is over nourished,
I grow with you.

You are the conch which reverberates the most celestial
hymns that swirls around with the incense smoke penetrating
deep into my soul producing the effect of moksha,
I cleanse myself with you.

You are the petal bed where I lie down with all my burdens
and challenges and worries and softly you start pouring as
marigold strengthening my pursuits then you turn to rose
and soothe away all my pain of unloved parts and as you turn

into lavender I start hearing the lullabies of my childhood
and eventually you cast the spell of deep slumber on me,
I Sleep with You.

You are the attire I wear, also the accessories. You drape
your threads of sparkling yarns over me with ease of molding
a deity following each step meticulously converting my
otherwise monochromatic persona into vibrant radiance that
mesmerizes my mirror and I see you twinkling as the solitaire
on my ears.
My fingers, you play hide and seek from my cleavage as the
chunky crimson ruby, perhaps my racing beats serves as your
timer,
I am beautiful with you.

# 111

Play a silent tune,
This would be heard only by me.
Paint a rainbow on my eyelids;
With colors collected from pansies and tulips.
Weave a gown of butterflies,
Adorn it with sequins of fireflies.
Wash my hair with dew drops,
Decorate it with thousand stars.
Carry me,
Into the chariot of cherries and plums,
Shower upon me the light of the moon.
Come,
Hold my hands,
Let's dance to the rhythm of rain.
Caress me with the depth of your eyes,
Smile a thousand sunshine,
Kiss me the eternal kiss,
And make me your destiny bride.
I do,
Do You?

# 112

What rhapsody gives birth to such rigmarole?
How germinates the seed so sweetened yet vicious?
When was the last time you saw the moon bow or did you
ever see it?
The pine shaded your head and the grass comforted your
feet?
How did you feel when you waltzed in the tune of the gentle
southern breeze?
Did you switch off all those artificial lights of your home and
bathe it in starlight?
Which was the way you chose to adorn with petals soft and
scented and would tread onwards to your dreams?
Did you brew the most imperfect broth and felt
extraordinary?
What made you scream at the sight of the candy man?
Your taste bud is already dripping honey,
Why jeopardize your life and play with fire?
How would you explain your insanity to million wagging
tongues?
Those thousand missives you wrote wouldn't be reread or
revised,

So what made you search the finest quill and dip it in that
ethereal ink?
Pardon me if I m wrong,
But it was only a small gesture,
You could have easily pulled out the arrow and give it back
to the angel with little wings and a tiny bow.
 It would have really saved you,
Saved you from searching the oyster
Underneath the deepest sea.

# 113

These tangy moments
When my heart tastes sour
And my eyes sprinkle salt
All the organs stirring emotions with zest
There I have a robust appetite for you.

Crispy shadows of gooey memories
Churns and splash all over
There I lay down and pick up the crumbs
Seasoned with patience
Beaten by fate,
I nibble the tidbits
From the platter of life.

## 114

Several times,
Several times she glides down
From her pedestal
Clinging pathetically
To the roots.
Forbidden thoughts,
Prick her mind incessantly.
She keeps on dodging the thorns
Like a professional.
And again like an amateur,
Falls flat like the autumnal leaves
To decay with hope to bloom again
To caress the summer breeze
With her gorgeous green.

# 115

On the realm of platonic perusal
I have fallen in love with your sheer magnificence
Pages have witnessed my anxious trembling fingers
Flattered just by the touch of your notebook..
So many times I gasped for air,
As I drowned in the unfathomable depths
Of your words and thoughts,
Lingered however for a minute or two
To die inside your poetry.
In bargain there would lay my soul.
Immortal;
In your creations.

116

There are some abominably
Strong sparkling strings
Which doesn't let your
Soul's spirit sink.
Like the ones that never fails to ask you
"Did you eat your meal?"
Or the ones that reminds you to drive safe
And notify once you reach home.
The ones that defend you even in your
Absence but reprimands your trivial folly.
Or the ones that never lose patience with you
When even you yourself feel like
Breaking a brick on your head.
The ones that understands your silence
More than your words,
Or the ones who invariably sends
Favorite song or a joke when you are at
Your sullen best, as if tied under some
Telepathic spell.

If you have one such string, tie the knot harder than hard.

117

My limp lingered on the hope of
Dancing again
Before the anesthetic slumber
Engulfs my senses,
The sterile room was filled with masks and the musky
Aftershave evaporating from the white coat
Was smelling of lilacs, freshly bloomed, drifting me
Towards the field of faith.

# 118

In spite the shackles, the fetters
This imprisonment of our desires,
The rights of vows suppress the bleeding hearts.
Yet,
We dared to weave our magic castle
On the fabric of sheer tenacity.
Our sighs mingle with despair,
Time to time.
Yet,
The phoenix inspires our unified souls
Again and again.

## 119

Slumber travels past the meadows
Ride beneath the canopy
Collecting spring's fragrances
Of roses and lilies
Swims with the swans
Sings along with the robins
Cuddles like polar bear
Limps like the penguins
Waltz with the peacocks
Plays with the nymphs
Adorn the tresses with shiniest stars
Wears taffetas and silks,
Sweet slumber proud of its dreams.
Suddenly a bitter pill,
It swallows
Like a reluctant child
Returns to my tattered pillow

120

Romance never goes unpunished
Love never is fair;
All that glitters may be not gold,
All that shines may not be rare.

Love may paint a rainbow
Love may carve a sea
It may blossom like cherries
On a thorny tree.

But it can be robbed of its fragrance,
Like a open perfume bottle loses its essence.
Or lose its taste like a cold sizzler,
Or like a china cup get chipped on some places.

To hold and to be held
To be told and to tell
Could make all the difference
Could turn into heaven from hell

*DESIRE*

201

All of the king
King and
All the magical moments
Enthralled
Whims and fancies take a toll
The unseen tears of the rag doll

The glitter of illegitimate carnival
Mercy shining brightly on virile galls
The uncertainty of the doll
Hidden undercover shall forever growl

# 202

They called my desire a sin
And my sin a habit.
Little did they know,
I was growing out of habit
To fulfill my desire
And most of the time
I loved to sin.

Juggling between love bites and meditation,
A holistic phase floats over skyscrapers.
Nonetheless sinners water their gardens
in hope to conquer spring,
While spring takes a sojourn at autumnal retreat.

Desires die hard they say
They are blind to foreseen myths
Lying in a pool  of blood
Bubbles are counted one by one
Stench and flies overbearing
It is ambiguously intoxicating
The desire to sin.

203

Existing in separate realms
Some common hopes
Some similar dreams.

A forbidden emotion,
That hurts and heals.

Invisible fetters
Of time and fate;
Desires that would never be met.

204

She rose from her own ashes
Burnt in several form of corpses
She cleansed away all the venom that was spat on her
Aphrodite she wasn't by birth,
Death made her so.

She could accumulate admirations with poise and grace
She sheltered honest praises
With expressionless countenance

She could surpass amorous glances
With dignity shining on her nose
She severed lustful leeches
Like thorns from the rose

She searched for divine depth
Seeked for a healing touch
She just couldn't withstand being jilted or forlorn
Bearing that was too much.

She melted in adoration
Diluted with love

She dusted her metallic cage
But her mind was a dove.

She tiptoed several times towards the unforeseen
Harbored sin in her bosom
Treaded where no one have been.

She created her own melody
Grew her own spring
Basked in her own summer
Her bonsai was evergreen.

She wasn't sculpted from foam
As was the myth,
She was burnt brutally
 Every flame charred her flesh and bone,
But it couldn't touch her soul,
She wasn't born as Aphrodite
Death made her so.

## 205

She was no sylph who mingled only in thoughts
The pulchritude of flesh, of blood,
Of passion and of emotional outbursts.
Polishing tips and toes,
Preserving wonder and woes

There she stands, caressing whirlwind in her bosom
Succumbed to your desire of her
Being the myrmidon.

She wasn't precarious about the love she holds-
Nothing gave her more certainty than this realization
Her existence breathes in this wedlock not through unison
But firm by separation…!!!

## 206

God forbid you're attracted to me
I need to keep my magnets alive
Faded jeans are daily wear
Torn books are archived.

On the slippery side of the brook
I stained the grass in vain
An everlasting quicksand was tied on my feet
Several miles were covered on memory lane.

Seeking patrons for web clearance
Faces on wall hums lullabies
Once upon a midnight dreary
I attracted demonic alibis.

207

Simplicity wakes up every night from her graveyard
Wanders along the concrete wood of materialism,
Meets and greets all her rivals and contemporaries,
campaigning for herself,
In vain!
Exhausted and jilted,
She vows to rest in peace
Goes back to her solitude,
To rise again the next day with a hopeful heart.
She waits for the day her resurrection
Would be acknowledged and celebrated,
Just one more time!!!

# 208

Emerald sails of my love boat
Combat the ruby rage meticulously
On the turbulent sapphire waves
Berserk with unfolding emotions that darted
The unrequited patches of gloom on the
Silvery moon to trace for posterity, mast of
Marshmallow, mellowed down to sapphire
Shine, splashes and thrashes continued till
The sail was washed away of all its emeralds.
Green and blue shared their disaster on the
Carcass of ruby,
The red.
The reason of the
Journey couldn't die, but the silvery moon denied,
Artists were already stroking with their rosy brushes.
A faint tune of 'row row your boat'
Played consistently on my grey head.
Reflection of the same smirked and
Silently proclaimed the sail has seen better
Emerald days and the sapphire too was deep
And docile.
Ruby tricked them all into this

Never ending journey of love.
Only moon was happy with the documentation,
Her silver was aware of the gold of the sun.
Now that's another chapter of unrequited love.

209

All I need is a little rain to cry
My wishbone couldn't trick my eyes
My little rain would suffice
My malady of dry dead eyes
If only I could get a little rain to cry
My momma called them pearl drops
Not to be wasted in vain
I plea her to recommend in her heaven
Nothing much, nothing more.
To send a little bit of rain.
Enough to drench my thirsty eyelids and
My frowning eyelashes
Just wish this desert feel diminishes

# 210

One who desires to be free?
Renders freedom to others
Constantly waiving off follies
So not to be blamed
Showering indifference
In disguise of leeway
Pretending to be liberal.
Eventually,
Progresses on the path
Of futile masquerade
Posing perfection virtually.
The key of happiness
Perhaps is to drift apart from
Reality.
So what of the onions cry when fate chops them?

# 211

Dusk and dawn were celebrating
Culmination of their entwined heart
After many thoughts, negotiations and
Promises,
They decided not to part.

Dawn made a pact with sun
Dusk requested the myriad stars
Sky was made the judge
Of this union bizarre.
Existing in separate time zone,
Belonging to opposite realms
A desperate wishbone waltzed
In unconventional rhythm and theme.

Moon weaved the bridal gown
Consent on the unbelievable event
Night looked dismayed and forlorn
Apprehending long term bereavement.

Thus came the big day of alliance
Dawn adorned herself in anticipation

On the other side of hemisphere
Dusk awaited the setting sun.

Zillions and zillions years after
They are still paused in time
The shooting stars are nothing but their
Cumulative teardrops,
Fulfilling wishes with their passion sublime.

## 212

Penetrating your rigid shell
With wealth of honey talks
Melted honey stuck on the tonsil
A housefly simply followed it
Cough, sneeze, and vomit after
The fly flew
And I knew
Too much sweetness scares you
Not because you wee diabetic,
But the shell that cocoons you was made up
Of sugar coated tongues
And honey dipped stabs.
You didn't require healing
So I made you feel
My caramelized sweetness
With needles and nails,
Both sterilized.
Now I live in your shell too,
Dulcet and at ease.

# 213

Lose me if you can
You would be harvesting your salt and pepper
Overgrown beard
Comb your shiny scalp
You just cannot lose me
Your fat thick lenses would still find me,
On your mirror,
In your playlist,
In your phone gallery.
Dare you lose me,
Even when you are losing yourself,
I would make you find me still,
In alarm clocks.

214

Exhilarating enliven visage
Give me your palm and I shall let you touch
Every molten pearl drop
Lend me your ears and listen
Pitter patter pitter patter
Symphony of water.

I drown in your eyes so many times
Which you are unaware of
I taste your salt,
I touch your spice,
You have sown in me the seed
Of eventual ecstasy.

Now I wish you to moisten your vision
With monsoon and moonlight,
Make you feel immortal
Your trust in serendipity
Ignited this flame of faith
See it through your senses.

The drizzling buzz on the tin roof

Penetrating through my eyes to yours
I have my own constellation
Weaved in your eyes
Navigate the wheels of the chair.

With your strong arms, as you maneuver our
Fortnightly waltz
I shall slide again in your chest
As you carry me to our rain dance
Soaked in your love,
I have given my wings to dry
To stand still and just be
Only your eye.

## 215

Carve that one moment
In your life
When you are tired of bliss
Let you lips bleed
Sow the sinner's seed
In darkness you glow
Let wilderness flow
Terminate all rituals and rules
Shut the decorum of fools
Unclasp your fetters
Let your spine feel the jitters
Feel the ecstasy of pain
Take a shower in the unholy rain
Drown into the dirty mud
Tear apart the innocent bud
In mirror when you see
You shall find a blossomed tree
In your life
Carve that one moment,
In your life
Don't repent.

# 216

There I sway as the blade of the grass
Just down your knee,
There you can see me.
The pigeon there that's fluttering its wings,
On the window pane,
I am in it too.
Holding you with my eyes,
Till I cry and you whoosh me away.
I am hanging on the bell to be rung.
You would touch the deepest chord and I
Wait for the warmth your touch would bestow.
Here and there,
There and forever
You can see me,
Only if you look.

## 217

A meager amount of emotion left
A pinch of hope
Your rigid demons nullifies
All the succulents to hold
Aftermath of colossal love
Perhaps nothing is left anymore
Salty waves wash away
Little footprints from the shore
Contrary to inner turbulence
Calm illuminated the lighthouse
Of faith and belonging
Of revival and surrender
The invincible desire to breathe in your strangle of love.

# 218

The hope remains
Of not being misunderstood
Of branches still adhered to their roots
A charming crystal of faith glows
To change the nightmare into a dream
To masquerade the burnt toast with layers of stale cream
There is a power in belief
Amen you said.
So did I,
For it's another story where
We can't see each other eye to eye.

# 219

You grew in me into thick foliage
You bloomed on a moonless wintry night
Sultry summers helped you grow
And you held on securely tight
Come spring my hope escalates.
For bouquets of fragrant petals
A sudden storm
And the uprooted feeling was fatal
Finger crawls desperately to hold onto the branches,
Relying on avalanches before,
But one can never hold back the adamant urge to go.

220

Dwindling in a prism of paradox
Confetti of snowflakes drizzle
Above all the tulips which was chosen
Summer smiles miles apart
Icy apocalypse of whatever humane
Frigid fingers point at the blue bells
Rigid steps gather carnations
Lawn mower mourns and rejoices
The tears of joy, the joy of tears
Layer after layer dandelion danced
And vanished into thin air
Hope they mingle with the sky at last
Bonsai poses as legal heir
Thorns in Roses executed yet the bleeding continues to turn
the night queens into crimson camouflage.
Jasmine sometimes fabricated its essence to lure humble bee
Floating in the nectar of immortality
Caterpillars initiate extinction of the butterflies.

# *DESTINY*

301

Whatever miles we walked together,
It was our road
Shades were own
Sun was kin
Blessings were far above
The sin.

Now that we walk apart
It's not that we don't turn back
And see
On the shades still lingers
Little of you
Little of me.

302

Sordid aftermath
Of morbid manifestation
Calamitous expeditions through
Itinerant cycle of forbidden love
Reproduces pungent aftertaste
On purple lips and palliative heart
Rotten reveries sail out on swan songs
Maneuvering cluster of unbridled temptations
Just to touch that one moment of complete nothingness....

## 303

We might forever stand
On opposite shores of the ocean
Watching the periodic turbulence
Pass one after another
Hoping for that one sail
That would transport us into each other's land.
For the time being
The waves shall be counted,
Every fall and rise
Would never be able to measure the depth of unfulfilled
love.

304

The 'Ludus' hours were spent in vain
You comforted your vanity
I lost my sanity
None of us parted with any gain.

'Eros' played its music in background
You retreated to our inglenook
I giggled like a brimming brook
A nouveau thrill we found.

The 'storge' of our lives retained
You cleared your mind
I hurt but couldn't find
Any reason to resent.

'Philia'now rules the show
You are the panacea of my story
I treasure our impeccable glory
The boat of destiny row.

305

Indifference arises from
Lack of responsibility
The heart targeted
Are left to wonder
The validation of existing
Seems immaterial
In so called forever bonds
Where even a minute
Of complete rendition
Is included in whatsoever
Expanded time of nothingness.

# 306

You say you don't know
I say the same too
Are we really that naive?

What does the mirror say?
What utters the soul?
Are we playing masquerade with our own selves..?

I sweep the crater inside me
Clean the dried up wounds
Lead to the path which would save

You hide your unknown pain
Laugh out loud to the crowded void
Perhaps what you got, doesn't compliment to what you gave.

What started as a fantasy,
Is a fact now.
Which would only succumb to grave.

# 307

You I know not,
Who sit amidst the wood
And read fairytales,
In a pensive mood.
I have crossed your brook,
Have touched your skin,
Colored your nails,
And thought your trees will be evergreen.
Taffetas and silks that you wore
Truly now makes me so bore.
The kettle that boils
Is known to me.
The hundred wobbly hands
Is bliss to see?
The brain that jiggles between
Arts, vernaculars and science
Is familiar of the womb
That it well defines
'You' in fairy tales have been stunk
'Her' I know for she runs around the circle

# 308

Lemony syrup that I gulp down
Giving my throat everlasting fizz
Glides down like a serpent
Reverberating its hiss
That would be my nemesis
Cold, slain and thrown
Talons let loose everywhere
There lies nothing to be called as own.

The perfumes would still spread fragrance
The stilettos would still shine
Creases and folds would still smell of iron
The shelves would show off the best wine.

That lemony syrup shall die
And get the color of saffron
You shall bleed while the kitchen knife kisses your fingers
And you would rub it on my stranded apron.

Than the moribund would deserve
A celebration of strife
Shall steer my palomino
Towards the desirable life.

# 309

Stood and felt- blood dripping
Ceaselessly- from back which held the spine
The strong, rigid, spine
Which was once mine?
The masquerades, the shams
The shameless, the ignorant
The immortals, all together-
They stabbed, thousand Brutus altogether
They pierced in with vengeance unknown,
Unaware of each other.
Crimson pool drowns me
Into oblivion- uttered a name
Did I?
While in an endless reverie, I slip
Was it your name along with a sigh?

310

Crimson on my forehead
Symbolically shines
The red syrupy delight
Beckons from the vines
The scarlet lips of the bride
Shimmers as she smiles
The cherubic fruit teases Eve
Alluring her to all guiles
The same 'Red' flows mercilessly
On the battle grounds
The braves, the innocent bathe
In the oozing gory wounds.

# 311

Severing the pages whose perusal is painful
Irresistible desire to burn it all
Those nonchalant echoes of sarcasm drool
Sedated under the oak that always stands tall
When one realizes the mutiny of mildews
Penetrating your soul
You turn into hemlock
And never answer any call.

312

The irony of fate
Was to hold the antithesis of life
In a strong grip of metaphorical semblance juxtaposed
between pause and action, silence and roar,
Assembled into a symphonic crescendo, unheard.
It was more a rattle of contaminated ribs,
Jingling an oxymoronic experience,
Where the sugar cube never dissolved in the cup of coffee.
Deep exclamation marks were spread
Throughout the forlorn journey,
Like milestones reflecting dead ends.
Yet, the strings produced melodic interludes
In serpentine movement,
Reverberating throughout the creation and annihilation.

# 313

From my dainty little hut

I could see his silvery yellow abode

His palace of sagas, epics and stories

Songs and lullabies too hold the fort


The threads of magnet he weaves

My iron heart magically weeps


My dainty hut forbids me to let in the breeze

The kettle whistles ominous warning

Finger entangles in the rosary

I see the milk burning.

Road that leads to your abode have up and downs

Some dilapidated milestones and a legit crown.


Years change, so changes myopic eyes of mine.

Your yellowish silver abode still entice

My soul travels every night through the prohibited road

Every night we pay the forbidden price.

# 314

Satin shroud of sin
My soft satin sin shroud
Loyalty to infidelity
Fidelity grey under cloud
In search of a lover
Landed on the lap of reformer
His fingers dig my fleshy mass
Several postmortems done on same carcass.

Silky cinnamon tresses flow
Flows my silky cinnamon tresses
Of peace and purity he sermons
In real, carves out hurtful places
He cuts with teeth
Heart's very beat
Chisel out whatever fairytale exist
My frail love knows not how to resist
Soft feather pillows laden with loads of guilt.

315

Are you seeking for loopholes?
To escape this dungeon which has become my synonym?
Are you gulping down the bitter pill which would keep you
alive but comes with a side effect of excruciating headache?
Are you finding it hard to resist this conscious dream which
doesn't let you sleep?
What is that makes you bring back the beast in you?
Why do I feel like deaf, dumb, blinds are fortunate?
And the dead are blessed!!??

You grow hemlock on your tongue
And expect me to drink the nectar
Which have scalded my inner self?
Still it's me failing every time..
How can you bury my breathing dreams?
They shall be immortal and would be haunting you in every
birth.

## 316

Those three letters and punctuation
You didn't even realize what it meant to me....
It was not just a word
It was my testimony
When I said or I heard from you
I seriously could hear violins too
Or perhaps a sarangi tune
Cool moisture shed from the eyes
Of my heart drenching my bosom
Which heaved heavily on some lost soul.
For the word was alive to me.
My dead skins replaced with radiance
Nothing was left to hear anymore
In your matter -of - the fact way,
You blew the three jewels away towards
The blackened fumes of a non emission done vehicle.
They may conjure strength and jump back
From my throat to lips.
But I fear you may not recognize them.
Those three letters and trillion emotions,
begrimed....

317

You left

With the right one

I still get confused by the greater than

Smaller than symbols

Shackles, fetters

In various forms entangle my feet

My throat,

I still am confused

Either to gasp for breath,

Or gulp down the lump that would

eventually push out from my eyes.

I tell you I m happy for your happiness

I am confused about my honesty

Confused severely about my existence with and without you

Who would tolerate her smiling?

While she walks away with the smile of your soul?

Now I m again confused about my generosity.

My kindheartedness,

But it's him, the savior of my soul, my muse

Who is leaving…

# 318

This imbroglio between
My heart and mind
Leads my soul to sink
In the unfortunate quagmire
Susceptible to withering
Into a termite who eats up
Self happiness with uncanny vigor
Under the oath of self destruction
Sprawling through epochs
As a twisted and tarnished
Crown.

# 319

New dimensions every night
Every night new hiccups
Last night's agenda was still lingering
Next night's slumber refuses to pick up
The sleep fairies as tiny white saviors
Already gulped down
Floating perhaps in the mid air
Enraging sleep with a frown
Every night the poetic lullabies
Inspires to sing the song of swan
Every night my slumber
keeps me hanging with incessant yawns.

# 320

Retreated to the nest where we lived in,

Contemplating a second chance.

We both carried our own keys

Entering to the Eden filled with the air of your musky
cologne was not a problem

But my nostrils hinted adulteration of a smell unknown,
mingled with the base fragrance....

Routed towards our slumber den,

 I halted at the dresser noticing the error in arrangement;

My beloved mascara was glancing away in guilt,

Confessed of curving other lashes.

A strong coffee would help to numb the investigative nerves;
I darted towards the laboratory of culinary exotica,

The sink there whistled at me enlightening my visionary
frailty,

Two coffee mugs waltzed in obscene disharmony,

 My once upon a time pink flaunted red lipstick stain
mocking my existence with fiery vengeance.

My valiant shoes galloped me away

From the pandemonium like a thunderbolt

Promising a one way ticket.

84

# ABOUT THE AUTHOR

Intoxicated by the smell of old books
Restoring, reliving and refurbishing.
Whatever is old.
Margins are for meekly
Marker is for the bold.

The author of the book, Reema Ghosh Majumdar, has done her Masters degree in English Literature, is primarily a 24/7 house mom of two lovely teenage daughters.

Writing is her childhood passion which is the only constant in her life. She is associated with several writing platforms. She also has her own Facebook page of poems by the name of 'Angelic Verses'. She is currently associated with an Anthology named 'Cashmere Diaries ', which compiles love poems by 12 versatile women writers.

She would like to be introduced as a 'Warrior of reality and weaver of dreams '.

www.ingramcontent.com/pod-product-compliance
Lightning Source LLC
Chambersburg PA
CBHW031216160726
47992CB00006B/2758